Stay Calm and Draw

Belongs to:

_____

Relaxing and decompressing are musts for self-care. Relax with drawing! This is the easiest drawing book available. There are pages for drawing horizontal lines and circles. Draw as many and few lines as you want. Draw small or large circles. Completely fill the page or not. It's all up to you!

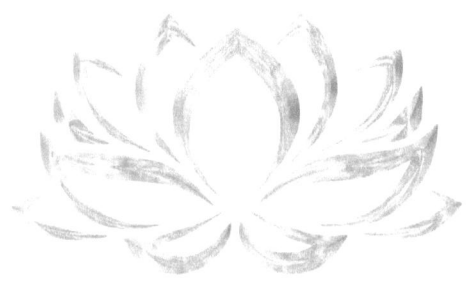

Calm Lines
Simply draw horizontal lines.

Calm Lines
Simply draw horizontal lines.

Calm Lines
Simply draw horizontal lines.

Calm Lines
Simply draw horizontal lines.

Calm Lines
Simply draw horizontal lines.

Calm Lines
Simply draw horizontal lines.

Calm Lines
Simply draw horizontal lines.

Calm Lines
Simply draw horizontal lines.

Calm Lines
Simply draw horizontal lines.

Calm Lines
Simply draw horizontal lines.

Calm Lines
Simply draw horizontal lines.

Calm Circles
Simply draw circles, big and/or small. See where it goes naturally.

Calm Circles
Simply draw circles, big and/or small. See where it goes naturally.

Calm Circles
Simply draw circles, big and/or small. See where it goes naturally.

Calm Circles
Simply draw circles, big and/or small. See where it goes naturally.

Calm Circles
Simply draw circles, big and/or small. See where it goes naturally.

Calm Circles
Simply draw circles, big and/or small. See
where it goes naturally.

Calm Circles
Simply draw circles, big and/or small. See where it goes naturally.

Calm Circles
Simply draw circles, big and/or small. See
where it goes naturally.

Calm Circles
Simply draw circles, big and/or small. See where it goes naturally.

Calm Circles

Simply draw circles, big and/or small. See where it goes naturally.

Calm Circles
Simply draw circles, big and/or small. See
where it goes naturally.

www.ingramcontent.com/pod-product-compliance
Lightning Source LLC
Chambersburg PA
CBHW030539220526
45463CB00007B/2904

*9 7 8 1 6 7 8 4 6 2 9 5 6 *